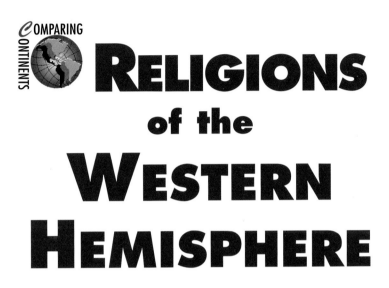

RELIGIONS
of the
WESTERN
HEMISPHERE

SUSAN DUDLEY GOLD

TWENTY-FIRST CENTURY BOOKS
A Division of Henry Holt & Company, Inc.
New York

I dedicate this book to my mother, Helyn R. Dudley, whose teachings shaped my life.

Twenty-First Century Books
A Division of Henry Holt and Company, Inc.
115 West 18th Street
New York, NY 10011

Henry Holt® and colophon are trademarks of
Henry Holt and Company, Inc.
Publishers since 1866

Published in Canada by Fitzhenry & Whiteside Ltd.
195 Allstate Parkway, Markham, Ontario, L3R 4T8

Library of Congress Cataloging-in-Publication Data
Gold, Susan Dudley
Religions of the Western Hemisphere / Susan Dudley Gold. — 1st ed.
p. cm. — (Comparing continents)
Includes bibliographical references and index.
1. North America—Religion—Juvenile literature. 2. South America—Religion—
Juvenile literature.
I. Title. II. Series.
BL2500.G65   1997
200'.97—dc21   97–30722
                                                                              CIP
                                                                              AC

Photo Credits
Cover photographs and photographs on pages 3, 6, 7, 14, 21, 25, 35, 46, 87, and 88 © PhotoDisc.
Illustrations on pages 12, 26, and 60 © North Wind Picture Archives.
Illustrations on pages 29, 37, 39, 49, 52, and 53 from North Wind Picture Archives.
Illustrations on pages 10, 33, 43, 57, 58, 70, 72, and 78 from the Collections of the Library of Congress.
Maps on pages 4, 17, 19, and 23 © 1997 Susan D. Gold.

Design, Typesetting, and Layout
Custom Communications

ISBN 0-8050-5603-3
First Edition 1997

Printed in Mexico
All first editions are printed on acid-free paper ∞.
1 3 5 7 9 10 8 6 4 2

CONTENTS

MAPS

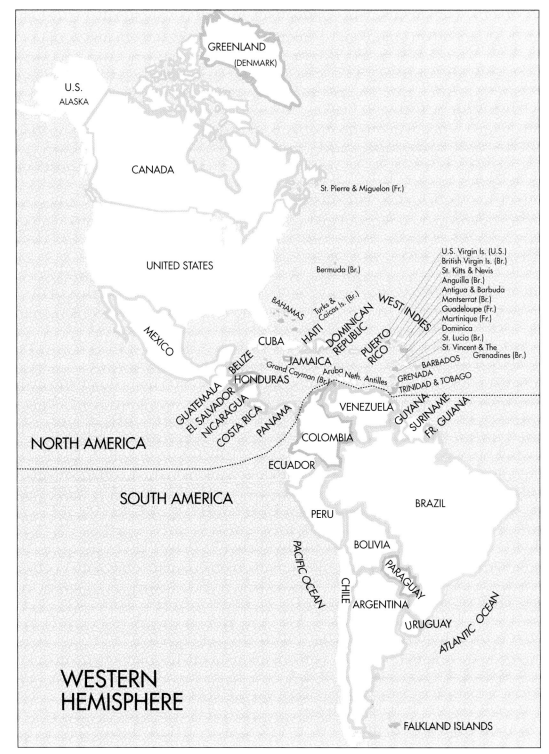

GREENLAND
(DENMARK)

U.S.
ALASKA

CANADA

St. Pierre & Miguelon (Fr.)

UNITED STATES

Bermuda (Br.)

BAHAMAS

Turks & Caicos Is. (Br.)

WEST INDIES

U.S. Virgin Is. (U.S.)
British Virgin Is. (Br.)
St. Kitts & Nevis
Anguilla (Br.)
Antigua & Barbuda
Montserrat (Br.)
Guadeloupe (Fr.)
Martinique (Fr.)
Dominica
St. Lucia (Br.)
St. Vincent & The Grenadines (Br.)

MEXICO

CUBA

HAITI

DOMINICAN REPUBLIC

PUERTO RICO

JAMAICA

Grand Cayman (Br.)

Aruba Neth. Antilles

BARBADOS

GRENADA

TRINIDAD & TOBAGO

HONDURAS

GUATEMALA
EL SALVADOR
NICARAGUA
COSTA RICA
BELIZE
PANAMA

VENEZUELA

GUYANA
SURINAME
FR. GUIANA

NORTH AMERICA

COLOMBIA

ECUADOR

SOUTH AMERICA

PERU

BRAZIL

BOLIVIA

PACIFIC OCEAN

CHILE

PARAGUAY

ARGENTINA

URUGUAY

ATLANTIC OCEAN

WESTERN
HEMISPHERE

FALKLAND ISLANDS

Source: *Britannica Atlas*

INTRODUCTION

PART OF THE FABRIC OF LIFE

From the earliest times, religion has played a central role in people's lives. This is as true in the Western Hemisphere as it is elsewhere. Thirty thousand years ago, the earliest settlers trekked over the frozen lands of the north across the Bering Strait to Canada, bringing their religious beliefs, their priests, and their gods with them. Centuries later, the empires of the Inca and the Aztec revolved around elaborate religious ceremonies and beliefs. The Pilgrims' desire to practice their religion freely brought them from Europe to North America. Roman Catholic priests set up missions throughout both continents to convert the native peoples, and, in some cases, to protect them from the greed and cruelty of adventurers seeking riches.

By the end of the seventeenth century, Christianity had become the major religion practiced by inhabitants of the Western Hemisphere. So great was Christianity's impact on the Western Hemisphere—and on today's world—that the universal calendar dates from the supposed birth date of Jesus Christ, on whose life the religion is based.

The teachings of Christianity and of the Jewish

Christmas, the Christian celebration of the birth of Jesus Christ, has become a national holiday throughout the Western Hemisphere.

faith (on which many Christian tenets are based) have been absorbed into the moral codes and laws of all the nations of the Western Hemisphere. Members of the Jewish faith were leaders in U.S. court fights to preserve freedom of religion.

Christian culture permeates the lives of practically everyone on both continents. In many nations, Sundays—the Christian day of worship—are, or have been, set aside as an official day of rest, when shops are closed and work is suspended. Christmas, the celebration of Christ's birth, is a national holiday throughout North and South America.

Many other religions, of course, have also had an

impact on the Western Hemisphere. Immigrants from all over the world brought their religious faiths and practices to North and South America. Rituals of the Western Hemisphere's Native American societies continue to inspire today's generations. Modern Western Hemisphere culture is a blend of many religious practices and beliefs.

What Is Religion?

Religion is a system of beliefs, usually linked to a belief in a supernatural being or beings who rule the universe. Judaism, Christianity, Islam, and other religions believe in one God. Many of the ancient religions practiced by the original inhabitants of the Western Hemisphere revolved around a belief in many gods.

Most religions believe in one or more lives after death. Some have a series of afterworlds, through which the dead must pass on their way to a final resting place. In many native tribes, gods represented various aspects of nature. Believers offered gifts—or sacrifices—to appease a particular god or to win favors. The Aztecs, an ancient civilization in Mexico and Central America, sacrificed human beings—usually captives from conquered tribes—to their gods. Other religions, strongly opposed to human sacrifice, offered crafted goods, food, animals, prayers, or spiritual chants as their gifts.

Some of the world's finest artwork and architec-

Above, a tiled shrine to the Virgin Mary

ture have been created for religious purposes. Elaborate temples and altars demonstrate the believers' devotion in many religions. In fifteenth century Peru, the Incas built huge palaces and temples, gilded in gold. Roman Catholics in the Western Hemisphere decorated their cathedrals with finely crafted statues, adorned the walls with dazzling paintings, and filled the altars with golden icons. New England Puritans, followers of a stern and austere faith, built simple, white wood structures for their worship.

Other religions, such as Hinduism, are centered on home and family. In these religions, followers often worship privately without attending a church or temple. Similarly, native tribes, especially those who wandered from place to place in search of food, often worshiped at outdoor spots.

While temples serve as the physical reminders of a religion, myths preserve its teachings. Myths are the stories carried down from one generation to the next that illustrate a society's beliefs. Most religions have creation myths or stories detailing how the world was made. World floods or fires, the origin of death, and the creation of crops or animals are common themes.

THE ROLE OF RELIGION

Religion has always tried to answer its followers' questions about life, death, and other matters of importance. It has attempted to explain natural disasters. Floods devastated the world because God was displeased with people's behavior, according to the biblical account of Noah's Ark. A similar tale is told in Native American myths.

People sometimes use rituals as a way of attempting to control nature. For example, in the spring, believers may offer a goat or other gifts to the god of rain to ensure a good growing season. Often rituals help people overcome their fear of death.

In some religions, people believe certain objects or charms contain power or influence with the gods. These objects, called fetishes, are often worn by believers who worship them. Totem poles are examples of other objects important in some Native American religions.

One of religion's most important functions, aside from its spiritual benefits, is its central role in keeping order and establishing a moral code for society. All religions have moral guidelines or laws that establish what is right and wrong. These religious rules are the basis of society's laws governing behavior.

Religion also performs another role, especially important for societies whose culture is threatened. Through its rites and rituals, its myths and sacred texts, religion preserves the history and culture of its people. For many of the defeated native tribes, retelling the myths of their ancestors was the one way they could keep their culture alive.

"We do not worship the church," noted a member of the Mexican Chatino tribe. "What we worship is the mountain and the sun stone [a hilltop shrine where

RELIGIONS

North America (cont):
St. Vincent and the Grenadines: 75% Prot., 13% RC
Trinidad and Tobago: 28% Prot., 32% RC, 24% Hindu, 6% Islam
United States: 56% Prot., 28% RC, 2% JD, 4% other, 10% none

South America:
Argentina: 2% Prot., 90% RC, 2% JD
Bolivia: 95% RC; also Evang. Meth.
Brazil: 90% RC
Chile: 11% Prot., 89% RC; also JD and Islam
Colombia: 95% RC
Ecuador: 95% RC
Guyana: 34% Prot., 18% RC, 34% Hindu, 9% Islam
Paraguay: 90% RC; also Mennonite and other Prot.
Peru: RC
Suriname: 25% Prot., 23% RC, 27% Hindu, 20% Islam, 5% indigenous (native)
Uruguay: 2% Prot., 2% JD, 66% RC
Venezuela: RC

Ang=Anglican Evang=Evangelical
JD=Judaism Meth=Methodist
Prot.=Protestant RC=Roman Catholic
Source: CIA 1996 World Fact Book and 1995 Information Please Almanac

At right, William Penn in 1682 negotiates a treaty to purchase land from the tribes who live in the area surrounding his colony in Pennsylvania.

people leave offerings], and that way we keep our Chatino rituals, beliefs, traditions, and stories."[1]

Religion—or at least people who acted in the name of religion—brought both good and evil to the natives who occupied the Western Hemisphere. The Europeans who introduced Christianity to the New World believed they gave a great gift to the "heathens" who lived there. Some native converts undoubtedly agreed. But many more resented the attempts to abolish their native religions.

Members of Roman Catholic religious orders, especially the Jesuits and the Franciscans, taught the natives to read and write, trained them as skilled artisans, and tried to protect them from the evils of slave labor.

Men like William Penn, a Quaker in North America, paid tribes a fair price for their lands and lived peaceably with their native neighbors.

Other Europeans, however, used religion for more sinister purposes. Spanish merchants and landowners in Latin America raided missions and seized converted Indians to work in their mines or their fields. In North America, Indians were converted to Christianity so they wouldn't attack European settlers, who claimed land that had been tribal property since ancient times. On both continents, people who had pledged to bring Christianity to the natives slaughtered them by the thousands in a quest for gold and land.

The lives of the first European settlers and those who followed were also influenced for good and ill by religion. Puritans in Salem, Massachusetts, fearful of witchcraft, hanged innocent men and women. Another group of Puritans established Harvard University and set up the beginnings of a public school system.

In today's world, observers often complain that we have lost touch with religion, that it no longer plays a role in our lives. This is far from the truth. History reveals that the religions of the Western Hemisphere—native and imported—are part of the fabric of life. Whether we are religious or not, religion influences our governments, our cultures, and the way we live our lives.

A. Bobbett Sc

CHAPTER ONE

THE FIRST WORSHIPERS

Long before Europeans began their mass migration to the New World, the native societies practiced their own religions. Many of these religions revolved around nature and the spirits believed to control humans' fate. There is no single Native American religion. In the 1400s before Columbus's fateful journey, more than two thousand native cultures existed in the Western Hemisphere. The religious beliefs and practices of these cultures varied widely, from simple nature rites to the elaborate ceremonial rituals of the Aztecs and the Incas.

NORTH AMERICAN INDIANS

The religions of the North American Indians revolved around a supernatural force that controlled nature. The Algonquins, in the Northeast, called this force *manitou*. The Dakotas, a tribe of the American

At left, members of the Ottawa tribe, who lived in what is now Michigan and Ontario, Canada, at a tribal council. Religious symbols, like the wampum belt held by the chief, played a central role in Native American rituals.

Plains, referred to it as *wakanda*. Other tribes believed the force existed as gods of the sun, moon, and earth. These beings or gods, who had human traits, rewarded people who pleased them and punished those who offended them.

The common belief that animals and plants were once human—or were spirits—led Indians to respect nature's creations. In some cultures, spirits were thought to occupy even rocks and trees. In northern tribes, religion dictated how and when to hunt and taught respect for the animals killed.

The Haida and other tribes in Alaska and British Columbia relied on salmon as their primary source of food. To them, the salmon was a sacred being that gave the shaman (Indian priest and healer) great spiritual powers. They believed every bone and every eye of the salmon they ate had to be returned to the sea so that the species would live forever.[1] Indians of the Southwest, where the economy was based on corn, had similar beliefs about the magical powers of their crops.

In some northern tribes, religion defined family relationships. Each family had its own totem, or emblem, usually in the form of an animal. Members of the family, or clan, were thought to be descendants of the animal represented by the totem. As a sacred being, the animal protected the clan members, who were forbidden to kill it. Those living under the totem were banned from marrying others within the same clan. They had to find a spouse among the members of another clan in the tribe.

Above, a totem pole in Victoria, British Columbia, Canada. Totems were believed to protect family members of some northern tribes.

FOUR WISHES

Gathered around blazing campfires, huddled against the cold Arctic wind, the people of the Wabanaki tribes in Maine and Maritime Canada tell of Glúskap, ancient god-hero and protector of the earth's people. Hearing of Glúskap's greatness, four men set out to find the god. Each has a wish he wants Glúskap to grant. The men struggle through the wilderness, trudging across frozen ground, bowed down by icy rain. Finally, they arrive at Glúskap's home.

As a reward for completing the treacherous journey, Glúskap agrees to grant the four wishes. He gives each man a pouch with the instructions not to open it until he arrives home.

The men set out in their canoes, but three of them can't wait to have their wishes come true. As soon as they are out of Glúskap's sight, they untie the strings of the pouches and release their wishes. The first man, who has asked to be the tallest person on earth, is turned into a tree. The second man, who has said he never wants to die, becomes a stone. Hundreds of gifts fill the canoe of the third man, who has asked to possess more than anyone else. The weight sinks his canoe and he drowns.

The fourth man, who has asked to be able to help his people, continues the journey alone. When he arrives home, he opens his pouch. It is empty. But suddenly his mind is filled with ideas. He discovers he knows what to teach his people so that they can improve their lives.

—A Wabanaki myth from *Parabola: The Magazine of Myth and Tradition*

Many tribes worshiped with the help of a shaman. He determined what the spirits wanted (often by going into a drug-induced trance) and told tribe members what they should do. Shamans often were believed to have the power to heal as well. The shaman led the tribe (usually the men) in rituals to prevent natural disasters, to guarantee productive crops or successful hunts, or to cure sickness. To ensure that the gods answered their pleas, the faithful fasted, danced, sang, and prayed. Certain cultures wore masks to scare away evil spirits. Each spring and fall, members of the False Face Society, an Iroquois sect, visited houses in the community, their faces hidden by masks carved from trees. During the ritual, they shook rattles made from turtle shells to protect against illness.[2]

In some cases, Indian worshipers underwent painful tortures to win favor with the gods. The Sun Dance, performed by the Plains Indians, was among the most dramatic rituals practiced by the tribes. Men who endured the three- or four-day ritual were thought to gain great power for their feat. The rest of the tribe watched the spectacular rite as the performers danced around a pole accompanied by drumbeats and song. During the dance, the most daring of the warriors pierced their skin and attached buffalo skulls to their bodies.[3]

Other rituals required believers to smoke tobacco or take drugs to put themselves into a trance. It was thought they could more easily contact the gods or enter the spirit world while in this state.

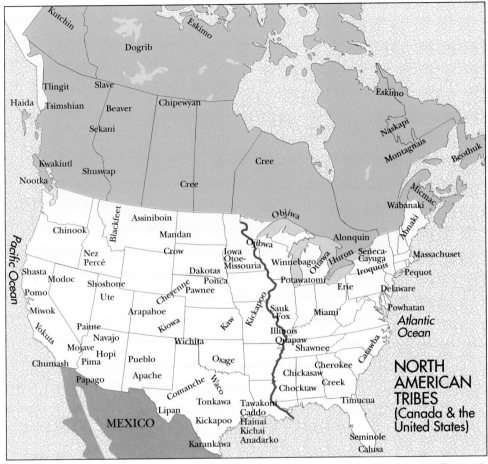

Sources: *Americans All* and *Compton's Encyclopedia*

Children often went through rituals to mark their passage into adulthood. The Hopi, a tribe in Arizona that continues to practice the ancient rituals, use the *kachina* doll, which represents a spiritual being in their religion. Children are taught that the kachina doll is a real being who gives gifts to those who are good and punishes those who misbehave. When boys and girls become more mature, they participate in the kachina ceremony. During this rite, they are introduced into the adult world and learn that the kachina is not real, but a representation of the spiritual world.[4]

Tribes performed ceremonies at a person's birth, marriage, and death. Most Indian cultures in North America shared a belief in a life after death. In some tribes, dead people's belongings were destroyed and their names never spoken lest they come back and harm family members. In other religions, tribes buried treasures, tools, everyday items, and food with their loved ones to help them in their journey to the next world. This ritual was so sacred that even starving Indians would never dig up the goods for their own use.[5]

Much of the Indians' worship occurred outdoors or in sacred huts, tipis, or caves. Some tribes centered their rituals in particular locations, such as the Black Hills in South Dakota. Some southeastern tribes used elaborate structures for their worship sites. Archaeologists working along the lower Mississippi Valley have found burial mounds for the dead and huge, flat pyramids of dirt on which temples had once been built.

AZTECS

When Spanish explorer Hernán Cortés arrived in Mexico in 1519, the Aztecs ruled most of that land and much of Central America. The Aztec religion was a brutal one that required huge numbers of human sacrifices to the gods who controlled nature. During one dry spell, Aztec ruler Montezuma II ordered the sacri-

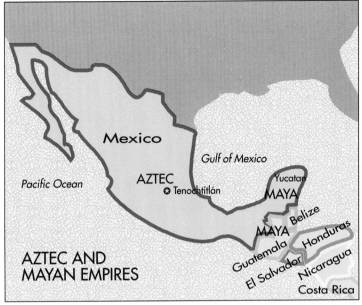

Source: *Latin America: A General History*

fice of twenty thousand captives to appease the rain
god.

Although the Aztecs first existed as a tribe around
1064, they had been at the height of their power for
only a hundred years or so at the time of the Spanish
conquest. Their religion was a mix of their own ideas
and the beliefs of other civilizations (particularly the
Mayas, Oaxacas, and Toltecs who flourished in the
area centuries before). According to Aztec belief, nine
gods ruled over the nine levels of the night (the un-
derworld), and thirteen gods oversaw the thirteen levels of the day or sky world (heaven).

The Aztec religion bolstered the goals of the political leaders. According to legend, the Aztec god Tetza-
uhteotl Huitzilopochtli (Magnificent God Humming

Bird on the Left) ordered Aztec leaders to unite the people in Mexico and Central America under their rule. In 1428, the Aztecs took over central Mexico and established a state religion to be followed by all the people under Aztec rule.

Fate played a major role in the Aztec world, and people had to humor the gods in order to survive. The Aztecs carried charms and practiced rituals to protect themselves from bad-tempered gods. They interpreted natural occurrences such as earthquakes as signs from the gods. Each segment of the society had a special god from whom they sought protection. Farmers prayed to the gods of the sun, rain, and corn, while fishermen and hunters prayed to their own gods. Even slaves had a god they believed could rescue them from their lowly position in life.

Everyone was expected to give offerings to the gods. Aztec priests used sharp reeds to cut their tongues, nostrils, or earlobes to offer blood during sacrificial rites. Rich Aztecs offered rubber balls (made from rubber trees in the region and especially prized), animals, herbs, or works of art. Merchants gave their slaves to be sacrificed, while warriors offered captives from defeated tribes. In the Aztec religion, the gift of life was the greatest offering that could be given to a god. The Aztec gods demanded human sacrifices; those who gave such sacrifices won great favor.

Twenty times a year, the Aztecs gathered at the base of the altar at Tenochtitlán, the capital city, for the presentation of gifts to the gods. Thousands attended these festive occasions. The priests' assistants dragged terrified prisoners from their cages and forced them up the steps to the altar. Below, drunken revelers cheered as they eagerly awaited the ritual killings performed by robed priests. The largest sacrifices occurred before Aztecs went to war.

The souls of people offered as sacrifices, along with those of women who died while giving birth and warriors, were given special places of honor in heaven. Others who died, the Aztecs believed, had to pass through all the underworlds. To complete the dangerous journey, a person had to ride on a dog's back across a raging river, escape arrows, and avoid crashing rocks and other dangers. The good eventually were ferried to safety. The evil were eaten or thrown into boiling water.

Every year at the dead feast, or *miccailhuitl*, the Aztecs paid tribute to those who had died. Today's Day of the Dead festival, celebrated annually in Mexico, traces its origins to the Aztec rite.

At the end of every fifty-two-year cycle, the gods decided whether they would destroy the world or allow it to continue. People put out all their fires, threw away old furniture and images of the gods, and fasted and prayed. When the stars moved to a certain spot in the sky, the grateful Aztecs held a huge celebration in honor of their renewed life. The high priest lit a new sacred fire on the chest of a sacrificed victim. Runners carried the flame to all the houses, where people relit their own fires and joined in the celebration.[6]

Above, a Day of the Dead display. During the festival, Mexicans honor the spirits of the dead. The holiday, celebrated on November 2 throughout Mexico, blends Christian and Aztec rituals.

The Incas ruled a vast realm that covered much of Ecuador, Peru, Bolivia, Argentina, and Chile by the 1500s. The empire absorbed smaller tribes in the region, adding the defeated peoples' gods and rituals to their own religion. An extensive system of roads and a universal language, Quechua, united the residents of the far-flung empire.

Incas believed the world was created by an all-powerful god, Viracocha. The sun and the moon were Viracocha's children (or brothers). Other Inca gods included Venus, Thunder, Earth, Sea, and the Dragon. The empire's first emperor, Manco Capac, was believed to have been the sun's offspring. All future emperors were said to be descended from the sun.

The emperor, or head Inca, ruled over the realm with an iron hand. He served as head of the government as well as of the religious life of the people. The Inca was so revered and so feared that people knelt as he passed by and avoided looking directly at him. He could have as many wives as he wished, but, under Inca tradition, he mated with his sister to produce the next emperor.

Like the Aztecs, the Incas believed that the gods wanted them to expand their empire. Soldiers were honored, and participation in military campaigns was seen as a religious duty.

Several times a day, Incas worshiped at temples, shrines, or open-air sites. The sun was at the heart of

the religion, with golden shrines dedicated to the sun god. Stone icons or sacred dresses commemorated dead loved ones and were thought to link the family to the gods. Each village had its own sacred mountain, on which residents placed a sacred stone (*huaca*) representing the mummy of the Inca who had conquered the town. Nearby, they placed other stones representing the people who had been conquered. The huacas were taken to the capital city of Cuzco during important religious festivals.

Priests presided over religious ceremonies and also served as healers. Incas brought gifts to the gods, usually gold, silver, flamingo feathers, and goats. Humans were sacrificed only rarely, perhaps at the beginning of military campaigns or at the crowning of an emperor.

At age eight or nine, the most beautiful girls were sent to special religious schools. For five years, they studied sewing, weaving, and the intricacies of performing religious rites. The best students were sent to Cuzco as attendants in the temples, where they assisted the priests and took care of sacred objects. To be chosen as a Virgin of the Sun, as the attendants were called, was a great honor.

The Inca religion was a practical creed, designed to help people make the best of their earthly existence. It outlined the behavior they had to follow to grow abundant corn crops and live peaceful, ordered lives.

A BLEND OF RELIGIONS

For four centuries throughout the Western Hemisphere, Spanish and French Catholic missionaries, and later English and American Protestants, attempted to convert the natives of North and South America to Christian faiths. As a result of their efforts, many tribes abandoned their native religions and adopted Christianity. Others—like the Hopis in the southwestern United States and the Araucanians of southern Chile—clung to their ancient rituals, which they continue to practice today.

Still others combined native rituals with Christian doctrine. Members of the Native American Church, for example, use peyote, a hallucinogenic drug derived from the cactus plant, to represent Christ's body during their communion observance. Church members live in Mexico, Saskatchewan, and southwestern and northwestern parts of the United States.

In Central and South America, many of the diverse religions practiced by the natives simply disappeared as the tribes died off or converted to European faiths. Yet some tribes managed to preserve their own culture even while adopting the new European religions. The result was a curious blend of Christian saints and Indian rituals, Catholic holy days and Indian gods. Traces of this blended religion can be seen today in many Latin American churches, especially during festivals.

Our Lady of Guadalupe is an example of this blending. According to legend, in December 1531 the Virgin Mary appeared in the form of an Indian girl to a poor Indian named Juan Diego. The vision occurred in Guadalupe, about four miles north of Mexico City, at the site of a shrine to the Aztec goddess Tonantzin (or Teotenantzin). Known as the mother of the gods, Tonantzin was revered as the goddess of healers and midwives. Years before the Spanish arrived in Mexico, Aztec believers visited the site to seek cures.

A church and a shrine dedicated to the Virgin Mary were built on the site of the apparition. In 1754 Pope Benedict XIV decreed Our Lady of Guadalupe as the national patron of Mexico and established December 12 as a Catholic holy day.

The shrine attracts huge numbers of visitors, especially among those with Indian ancestors, who come seeking cures to illnesses. Some of the native worshipers still call the holy figure Tonantzin.[7]

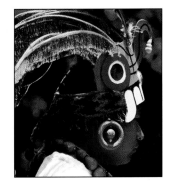

Although many Latin American natives converted to Roman Catholicism, others retained the customs and rites of their Indian religions. Above, a Mayan dancer.

EUROPEANS IN THE NEW WORLD

When Christopher Columbus first spied land after his grueling trip across the Atlantic, he named it San Salvador (Holy Savior) out of respect for his Lord. Claiming the territory for Spain, Columbus opened up a new world for Spain's Catholic missionaries. At least five priests accompanied Columbus on his second journey west, poised to begin a new crusade spreading the Catholic Christian faith among the natives in the new land. The natives—Columbus mistakenly called them Indians because he thought he had reached the East Indies—had their own religious beliefs, of course. Columbus, however, unable to speak their language and unfamiliar with native culture, saw them as heathens in need of conversion. "I believe that they would easily be made Christians, as it appeared to me that they had no religion," the explorer wrote in his journal.[1]

At left, a Spanish monastery in California. Beginning in the early 1500s, Roman Catholic monks and friars set up missions throughout Spain's New World colonies.

The natives resisted the Europeans' attempts to convert them to Christianity, but they soon learned resistance was futile.

Latin American Missions

In Mexico, Spanish conquistadors, equipped with guns and aided by the Indian enemies of the Aztecs, quickly crushed the Aztec's military empire. Roman Catholic monks, horrified by such religious practices as human sacrifice, destroyed Aztec relics and artwork and Mayan manuscripts in an effort to eradicate what they viewed as evil cults. Even in their revulsion, however, a few learned monks faithfully recorded the religion their brothers strove to destroy.

In South America, the mighty Inca civilization ended quickly in 1532 when Spanish explorer Francisco Pizarro and his men captured the head Inca. The once powerful ruler tried to buy his freedom with gold and silver. The Spaniards took the riches and baptized the Inca. But instead of freeing him, they put an iron collar around his neck and strangled him to death. Spain claimed the Inca lands.

Spaniards in Roman Catholic orders, in particular the Jesuits and later the Franciscans, soon set up missions to convert the Indian population. Their efforts extended from California and the southwestern United States to South America. The monks and friars transformed the native civilization into an agricultural society, with the Indians—converted to Roman

Catholicism—living much like the serfs of Europe during the Middle Ages. The friars taught the natives to farm, raise livestock, and tan hides. Their lives were regulated by the bells of the mission chapel, whose ringing called the Indians to work in the morning, to meals, and to evening worship. The missions resembled communes: all shared the work; all had their needs taken care of. The land and any profits from traded goods belonged to the mission.

The Jesuits and other orders set up missions throughout Central and South America, beginning in the mid-1500s. Soon Roman Catholic archbishops and bishops made their way to Latin America to serve the growing Spanish population and oversee the work of

Above, Spanish soldiers, overseen by a Roman Catholic monk, destroy the altars and religious statues of the Aztecs.

the missionaries. By 1600, five archbishops and twenty-seven bishops were stationed in the New World.[2] But priests, who served local parishes, were in short supply. To ease the shortage, the Pope allowed friars and monks to assume many of the duties of priests, including administering church rites to the tribes they converted. Often, they worked along the frontier, in isolated areas far removed from church offices and control.

The worst of the missionaries abused their power, exploited the Indians, charged fees for their services, and accumulated wealth. The best converted thousands of Indians and protected them from greedy landowners and mine operators looking for slave labor. In both cases, the church acquired vast holdings. By the 1800s, the Catholic Church controlled almost half of the productive lands in Latin America.[3] A million or more converted Indians farmed the land and performed other work. In return, the missionaries taught them skills, helped them sell their products, provided them with medical care, and educated them.

The Jesuits were particularly successful in Paraguay, Argentina, and Brazil, where in the early 1600s they organized one hundred thousand natives in almost fifty villages. Their work was not applauded by everyone, however. Rich Spaniards viewed the huge Indian enclave with suspicion and envy. They wanted the Indians to work in the mines; they longed for the gold lavished on the mission churches. Slave hunters raided the villages and snatched as many as sixty thousand Indians.[4] Finally, the Jesuits armed their Indian charges and taught them how to defend their villages against attack.

By the 1700s, the Jesuit villages had established their own governments, built roads, and set up a profitable trade in crafted goods, cotton, tea, and wool. Their success eventually led to the order's downfall. Members of other orders, jealous of the Jesuits' power, spread vicious rumors that devil-worship and sexual misbehavior were being practiced by the missionaries.

In 1750, the Treaty of Madrid divided the Jesuit villages into two segments, controlled by Spain and Portugal. When officials came to enforce the treaty, the Jesuits and their armed Indian converts fought off the armies of both nations. That action further built the case against the Jesuits. In 1759, Portugal expelled the Jesuits from Brazil after charging the members of the order with trying to assassinate the Portuguese king. Spanish King Carlos III issued a secret order in 1767 to remove the order from Spanish colonies as well. France, Austria, and Sicily followed suit, ordering Jesuits to leave their soil. In all, fifteen hundred Jesuits were ousted from America.[5] Under pressure from the world's Roman Catholic nations, Pope Clement XIV disbanded the order in 1773. It was later restored in 1814 by Pope Pius VII.

The expulsion of the Jesuits had a major impact on the Indians in the New World. As soon as the Jesuits left, the Indian villages in Latin America were destroyed. Some Indians were forced to work for the

Spanish mine owners. Others escaped and resumed their tribal religions. The action also turned the Jesuits against Spanish and Portuguese rule. In the years that followed, the black-robed religious leaders took a leading role in the fight for independence.

BLACKS IN LATIN AMERICA

The Spanish and Portuguese conquistadors brought a few black slaves with them on their expeditions to the Western Hemisphere in the early part of the sixteenth century. But the native Indians provided most of the slave labor used on the Europeans' farms and mines. In little more than sixty years, however, large numbers of Indians died from overwork and European diseases such as measles and smallpox, to which they had no immunity.

Huge plantations in Brazil had developed a booming sugar industry by the 1570s. The landowners, who had come to Latin America from Spain and Portugal, where the use of slaves was an accepted fact of life, turned to West Africa to solve their labor shortage. By the first half of the seventeenth century, Portuguese slave traders were bringing four thousand Africans a year to Brazil to work as slaves.[6] African slaves came in similar numbers to work in the gold mines of Colombia, the cacao fields of Venezuela, and the cattle ranches of Argentina.

Though many Roman Catholics opposed slavery, the church itself did not ban the practice. It did, how-

ever, oppose the inhumane treatment of slaves. Some friars and priests ministered to the African slaves, but on the whole the effort was not as vigorous—or as successful—as the missionary work among the Indians.[7]

The conversion of Latin American blacks to Roman Catholicism happened gradually and was achieved mainly through intermarriage with Indians and those with Spanish blood. Most Latin American nations abolished slavery by the mid-1800s; Brazil was the last to free its slaves, in 1889.

The descendants of black slaves overwhelmingly adopted Catholicism as their religion, but many combined the rituals of their new faith with the rites and beliefs of their African heritage. The African god Oxala became Jesus Christ; Iemanja, goddess of the sea, was transformed into the Virgin Mary.

Another remnant of blacks' African past is the belief in voodoo, most prevalent in Haiti. Voodoo combines elements of Catholicism and African rituals. Similar practices are found in Santeria, a Caribbean cult, and Candomblé and Macumba, Brazilian religions.

Voodoo worshipers believe in an all-powerful god and a collection of spirits, or *loa.* The loa rule over natural phenomena, such as fire, wind, or water, and are often linked to Catholic saints. Holy men conduct ceremonies designed to contact the spirits. Music and dance put believers into a trance, during which the loa enter their bodies. In that way, they communicate with the spirits and find out what actions they should take.

ROMAN CATHOLICS IN NORTH AMERICA

The French traders and explorers of North America, like the Spanish conquistadors, brought priests and missionaries with them to the New World. The Jesuits, in particular, saw the new land as fertile soil for their religion.

Jean de Brébeuf was among the first five Jesuits to travel to Quebec in 1625. He spent the rest of his life working to convert the Hurons, a tribe living in the Great Lakes region, to Roman Catholicism. As a result of his work and that of others, the Hurons remained French allies throughout the many conflicts between the French and the English. De Brébeuf died at the hands of the Iroquois, a rival tribe that supported the English.

The French viewed the work of the Catholic missionaries as an important aid in their battle with the English over North American lands. Missionaries were expected to win the Indian tribes as allies and keep them from siding with the English.

The strategy ultimately failed. With the Treaty of Utrecht in 1713, the Treaty of Paris at the end of the French and Indian War in 1763, and the sale of the Louisiana Territory to the United States in 1803, the French lost all claim to North America. Although the French missionaries had baptized thousands of Indians into the Catholic faith, a large number of them reverted to their own tribal faiths. Among the pockets of French settlers in New Orleans and Quebec, however, French Catholicism maintained a hold on the North American population.

Spain claimed much of the southern part of North America, including Mexico, Central America, and the American Southwest and parts of the South. As in South America, Spanish Roman Catholics established missions throughout the area to bring the teachings of Christianity to the native populations. Between 1769 and 1845, the Franciscans established twenty-one missions in California and baptized one hundred thousand natives.[8]

Above, a Spanish mission in California

PROTESTANTS IN NORTH AMERICA

A Protestant chaplain accompanied the members of the Virginia Company on their historic journey to the Western Hemisphere, where they established the first permanent English settlement in the New World, in Jamestown, Virginia, in 1607. Almost as soon as they landed, the adventurers knelt and celebrated Communion, a Christian rite that was administered by Vicar Robert Hunt. Hunt was a priest in the Protestant Church of England (also called the Anglican Church).

The settlers believed that people needed the guidance of the church and that they should bring the teachings of their Anglican faith to the New World and its inhabitants. But their main goal was to make a profit from their Western Hemisphere venture.

Nevertheless, they supported the church, setting aside lands to pay for the church's upkeep and the ministers' needs. Alexander Whitaker, an Anglican clergyman who arrived from England in 1611, persuaded the Indian princess Pocahontas to join the church. She was baptized and married colonist John Rolfe in an Anglican ceremony.

Laws enforced the role of the church. Colonists were required to attend daily morning and evening prayer services. Officials punished those who wore immodest clothes, bet, became drunk, swore, or were idle. People who continued to act bad could be jailed and have their church membership taken from them.

Under early laws, towns were required to educate a certain number of Indians. No such requirement, however, applied to blacks, who were brought to Virginia as slaves beginning in 1619 to help harvest tobacco. The Virginia farmers, who relied on slave labor to harvest their crops, considered blacks "creatures of another species who had no right to be instructed or admitted to the sacraments."[9] A Virginia law passed in 1667 noted that even if blacks were baptized, it would not change their status as slaves.[10]

Soon after the Jamestown group landed, English Pilgrims brought their faith to the New World. Before landing at Plymouth Rock in Massachusetts in 1620, the Pilgrims aboard their ship the *Mayflower* drew up a compact that described their undertaking as being "for ye glorie of God, and advancemente of ye Christian faith, and honour of our king & countrie."[11]

The Pilgrims were followers of an offshoot of the Puritan sect (which itself was an offshoot of the Church of England) who had fled from England to Holland after breaking with the Church of England. Though not persecuted in Holland, the small church wanted to go to the New World to establish an English community of its own. North America offered both land and separation from England's persecutions. William Brewster, one of the leaders of the Plymouth settlement, taught religious lessons on Sundays until a minister arrived from England in 1629.

English Puritans arrived in Massachusetts in the 1630s, establishing the Massachusetts Bay Colony. Unlike the Pilgrims, the Puritans considered themselves to be members of the Church of England. They believed in a stricter doctrine than that practiced by the mainstream church. The Puritans came to America hoping to set up a purer form of the Church of Eng-

Above, a Pilgrim couple on the way to church

land than the one they had left behind. They believed their New World community would serve as an inspiration and model for what they viewed as the corrupt church in England.

The English Pilgrims and Puritans saw the New World not so much as a source of converts but as a fertile ground where they could plant their religious community. English missionaries converted some of the original inhabitants to their Protestant faith in part because Protestant England wanted to prevent a Catholic take-over of the Western Hemisphere.

In the 1600s Puritan missionaries like Thomas Mayhew and his grandson Experience Mayhew converted northeastern Indians to Protestantism, organizing the faithful into villages. They were known as Praying Indians because of their devotion to the faith. For the most part, however, the British persuaded tribes to support them through trade rather than religion. In fact some British settlers believed the Indians had no souls. These new settlers' demand for land soon sparked conflicts that ultimately would drive the native tribes from their homelands.

Eventually the Puritans broke with the Church of England and merged with the Pilgrims. They formed the Congregational Church and did away with the hierarchy of bishops and other high Church of England officials and much of the pomp associated with Anglican services. The people, or congregations, of each church appointed their own ministers. They saw their church as a purified form of Anglicanism. They be-

lieved in a stern moral code, which emphasized the importance of hard work, self-reliance, and civic responsibility. Puritans believed that those who lived by this rigorous code would go to heaven.

New England Puritan towns looked much like English villages, with a town square and the church in the center. The church was at the center of the settlers' lives as well. New Englanders socialized with friends and neighbors at the plain, white meetinghouse, where both church services and civic meetings were held. The preacher gave long sermons and led the congregation in prayers and the singing of psalms at morning and afternoon services that filled most of the day on Sundays. Church members were also expected to attend a religious lecture on Thursdays.

Leaders in the community were active in the

Above, Pilgrims worship in Plymouth. The lives of the North American Pilgrims and Puritans revolved around the church.

church. Their seating in the front of the church reflected their status. At town meetings, selectmen voted on the minister's salary and arranged for the upkeep of the meetinghouse along with road repair and other civic matters. Ministers, often the most educated and learned men in the community, advised officials on civic matters. Religious leaders helped fashion laws; courts consulted the Bible as the final authority on legal points and to determine which crimes warranted death sentences.[12]

The Massachusetts Bay Colony had become a commonwealth in 1632 and elected its own governor and local officials, but only church members were allowed to vote. Even so, fewer than 20 percent of the population were official church members.[13] A ruling by Bay Colony leaders in 1635 stipulated that only those adults who had had a personal call from God were allowed to become members in the church. Everyone, however, was required to set aside Sundays as a day of rest and religious contemplation. Those who failed to follow the tenets of Puritan doctrine were whipped, hanged, or exiled. The Puritans, themselves once scorned by Church of England traditionalists, allowed no dissent. They believed they did God's will by requiring the entire community to support the church.

SEEKING RELIGIOUS TOLERANCE

Despite the harsh treatment meted out to those who did not follow the church's teachings, several of the early settlers objected to Puritan rule. Dissenters—those who did not agree with Puritan doctrine—fled the early colonies and built their own communities. There they practiced their versions of the Protestant faith. Some allowed other dissenters, even those who did not follow the same faith, to share their new home.

Roger Williams, a young Welsh preacher who had arrived in Boston in 1631, established a haven for all religions in Rhode Island after he was ordered to leave the Bay Colony in 1635. Puritan leaders objected to Williams's call for religious freedom. According to the document setting up the commonwealth of Rhode Island in 1647, everyone was required to obey civil law but all people "may walk as their consciences persuade them, every one in the name of his God." [14]

On March 16, 1639, Williams founded the first Baptist Church in America, in Providence. He later left the church, but the Baptist movement took hold and spread rapidly in the following century.

Another Bay Colony dissenter, Anne Hutchinson, began preaching her belief that God made his presence known to true believers. These "chosen ones" had the ability to identify others who had direct communication with God, according to Hutchinson. The ministers and religious leaders of the community, however, were not necessarily on Hutchinson's list of chosen ones. Condemned for her views, Hutchinson was banished from the Bay Colony in 1637. She eventually fled to Rhode Island, where she was welcomed. Because of Rhode Island's role as a refuge for dissenters,

THE SALEM WITCH TRIALS

Residents of seventeenth-century New England lived in a world peopled by ghosts, witches, and wizards. When mysterious things happened, they blamed the devil.

So it was in the spring and summer of 1692 in the Puritan town of Salem, Massachusetts. A group of adolescent girls who spent the long afternoons at the home of the Reverend Samuel Parris began to act strange. They spoke bizarre words and went into trances. Ministers and the local doctor who examined them decided they had been bewitched. Hysteria spread through the town. Town and church officials grilled the girls until they named those who had cast spells on them. They pointed the finger at upstanding members of the community: housewives, workmen, farmers. Neighbors who held grudges against other neighbors pressed their own charges.

The defendants were brought into court in chains with no lawyer to defend them. One defendant, the Reverend George Burroughs, was brought to trial after several accusers said his spirit had tormented them. Burroughs, a Harvard graduate, had served as minister in Salem in the early 1680s before transferring to a church in Kittery, Maine.

During court testimony, Burroughs's accusers said the minister's spirit had tried to force them to sign the devil's book and had bitten them, leaving teeth marks on their skin. One girl said he had carried her to a high mountain and had promised her "mighty and glorious Kingdoms" if she agreed to write in the book. Another said she had seen the ghosts of Burroughs's two dead wives, who claimed he had murdered them. Several others confessed to being witches themselves and testified that Burroughs had lured them into witchcraft by promising to give them fancy clothes. They said the minister gave them puppets which he taught them to stick with thorns to put curses on other people.

Burroughs vehemently denied all charges against him. Nevertheless, the jury found him guilty and sentenced him to hang. As he stood at the gallows, he recited the words of the Lord's Prayer in a clear, resounding voice. It was thought that witches could not utter the prayer, but the hangman put Burroughs to death anyway.

The witch trial of George Jacobs

Religious leaders, including Cotton Mather, the well-respected minister of Boston's Second Congregational Church, encouraged officials to hold the trials. Jurors were all church members. Few dared to oppose the proceedings. Those who did were accused of being witches themselves.

As the trials wore on, leading ministers began to question the validity of testimony based on spirits that no one but the accuser could see. Cotton Mather called for an end to the proceedings in a sermon to his congregation. With support from the clergy, the governor of the Massachusetts colony freed the accused and stopped further executions.

Before the hysteria ended in September, Salem authorities hanged nineteen people and pressed one man to death with stones. In New England, a total of forty people lost their lives during the witch-hunt. The episode shamed religious leaders and weakened their hold over their congregations. As serious as the New England witch trials were, however, the situation was far worse in Europe, where thousands of people were burned at the stake or hanged after being accused of witchcraft.

—From *A Documentary History of Religion in America to the Civil War*

Puritans viewed the new commonwealth as the "sewer of New England."[15]

Though the Puritans held power over most of New England for more than a century, European migrants to North America soon established their own Christian faiths in neighboring territories. The renowned Quaker William Penn created a refuge for followers of his faith and other religions in Pennsylvania in 1681, while George Calvert (Lord Baltimore) brought his flock of Roman Catholics to Maryland in the 1630s. Swedish and Dutch settlers in New York established the Lutheran Church and the Dutch Reformed Church, both Protestant sects, in that region.

Each ethnic group brought its own language and culture to the New World settlements, and each followed its own faith. By the mid-1600s, more than twenty languages were spoken in New York alone.[16] Eventually, there were so many different religions in North America that no one sect could claim control.

In 1684 the English government took away the Bay Colony's status as a commonwealth, and made it a royal colony in 1691. The new charter restricted the vote to citizens who were property owners rather than church members. The charter also limited the church's power and required citizens to be tolerant toward Anglicans, who had established a center in Boston. A new class of rich merchants began to assume power that had once been held by the Bay Colony's Puritan religious leaders. The hysteria and hanging of witches in Salem and other towns in 1692, which ended after supernatural evidence was discounted, further eroded people's respect for the Puritan leaders.

William and Mary, who served as England's joint monarchs, issued a Declaration of Toleration in 1689 that made it illegal in England to persecute people because of their religious beliefs. This move to religious tolerance came slowly to England's North American colonies. For example, the New York governor arrested Presbyterian minister Francis Makemie in 1706 for preaching without a license. The governor, however, was later recalled to England for violating William and Mary's edict.[17]

Geography, not intolerance, proved a major obstacle to churches in the South. There most of the population lived on plantations far removed from each other. The few trained ministers had to travel long distances to serve their followers. The Anglican Church was the most successful in the region, mainly because it had the financial support of the government. Of the forty-three thousand Anglicans in the North American colonies in 1701, twenty thousand lived in Virginia and another twenty thousand were from Maryland.[18]

CHAPTER THREE

REVIVAL AND REVOLUTION

As the colonists in North America headed into the eighteenth century, many had become complacent about their religion. New England churches, in particular, followed a formal ritual that had changed little over the years. Sedate ministers droned on for hours. Attendance dwindled.

This all changed with the sermons of Jonathan Edwards and others who followed his lead. These new ministers freed the emotions of their listeners; they inspired them with fiery words.

Edwards preached most of his career at the Congregational Church in Northampton, Massachusetts. He believed that only through God's grace could people be saved from hell. During his sermons—and in his numerous essays—he described in terrifying detail the punishment awaiting sinners and the joyous salvation of the soul.

At left, a statue of Christ stands watch over Rio de Janeiro, Brazil. Though the Roman Catholic Church was closely identified with the colonial rulers of Latin America, the people overwhelmingly clung to the faith during and after the Wars of Independence.

Eager to hear the exciting speeches, people packed the churches of New England beginning in 1734. The most exuberant preachers boomed out judgments against the wicked and told of the glories of God. Many in the congregation, overcome by emotion, burst into tears, fainted, or shouted their approval. This was far from the staid and formal Puritan service of yesteryear.

Edwards was joined by another extraordinary orator, George Whitefield, an Englishman trained as an Anglican minister. Whitefield came to America in 1739 when he was twenty-five years old, determined to improve a church that he believed had become too lax. Whitefield at first spoke to overflowing congregations in churches in Georgia, New York, and Pennsylvania. In 1740, he traveled to New England, where he would have his greatest success. From the pulpit in King's Chapel in Boston, Whitefield exhorted his listeners to mend their ways. The New England clergy, fed up with the young preacher's criticisms of their ministries, soon barred him from their pulpits. He took his message to the masses, in rented halls and open fields. On October 12, 1740, a crowd of thirty thousand people gathered in Boston Common to hear the young English preacher. They were not disappointed. "Whitefield," wrote one observer, "was an event." [1]

Benjamin Franklin wrote of the "extraordinary influence" of Whitefield's sermons on the masses who crowded into the fields to hear him. "It was wonderful to see the change soon made in the manners of our in-

habitants," wrote Franklin, after witnessing a revival meeting. "From being thoughtless or indifferent about religion, it seem'd as if all the world were growing religious."[2]

Indeed, the churches of New England and elsewhere in the English colonies thrived in the wake of the revival, called the Great Awakening. Inspired by the fervor of Whitefield, Edwards, and others, New Englanders established one hundred and fifty new Protestant churches, mostly Congregational, from 1740 to 1760.[3] As many as fifty thousand new members joined churches in this era.[4]

Baptists, Methodists, and Presbyterians also flourished in the second half of the century. In 1740, only twenty-one Baptist churches existed in New England; by 1768 that number had increased to sixty-nine. Before the end of the century, almost three hundred

Baptist churches preached to more than seventeen thousand New England faithful.[5]

Even Anglican churches increased their membership, mostly from among those who disapproved of what they viewed as a "reckless, emotional binge."[6] Liberals, who favored a more rational approach to religion, also turned to the Universalist and Unitarian churches. Although the revival was strongest in New England, itinerant (traveling) preachers carried its message to churches in the South as well.

In addition to boosting church membership, the revivalist movement spurred efforts to convert the Indians and to support higher education for both native and colonist. Eleazar Wheelock, an enthusiastic supporter of the Great Awakening, established the Indian Charity School in Connecticut in 1754 to train Indian boys to be ministers to their people. The school moved to New Hampshire, opened its doors to English colonists, and became Dartmouth College. Ministers also trained at Brown University, founded by Baptists in 1764.

As the century wore on, religious fervor waned. Colonists were diverted by the French and Indian War in 1763 and by revolution in the following decade. But the momentum of the revival movement helped build the foundations of many Protestant denominations. It also reintroduced religion as a vital part of American life. According to religious historian Richard Bushman, the Great Awakening was "a psychological earthquake [that] had reshaped the human landscape."[7]

At the end of the French and Indian War in 1763, England gained control of all of Canada and all North American lands east of the Mississippi River except Florida and New Orleans. The Protestant king soon decreed that the Church of England was the official church in the new territory and ordered that schools be set up to teach children the doctrines of the faith.

The colonists in the territory that would soon become the United States of America had no intention of allowing the English to dictate their religion or anything else, for that matter.

Within twelve years, fed up with British taxes and government in which they had no say, the colonists revolted and formed a new nation. Colonial ministers played an important role in rousing the population against the British. In 1772, John Allen, a Baptist minister who had recently migrated from England, delivered his powerful "Oration on the Beauties of Liberty" to the congregation of the Second Baptist Church in Boston. That sermon and others, published in pamphlet form, soon made the rounds and helped unite colonists in their fight against English control.

The American Revolution gave the triumphant colonists the freedoms they sought, including the right to practice their own religions. Eventually, a remarkable constitution established a unique government controlled by the people. When George Washington took office as the nation's first president, he wrote to

Above, George Washington is inaugurated as the first U.S. president in 1789.

assure Baptists, Jews, Roman Catholics, and Quakers that the United States would give to "bigotry no sanction, to persecution no assistance."[8]

Several of the new nation's leaders, including Washington, were deists, who believed in God but did not accept the teachings of any established church. The appointment of a state church, they believed, would threaten the nation's newly won independence. Quakers, Mennonites, Amish, and other groups opposed to the use of force also took a strong stand to separate church from state. This was a revolutionary idea, however; all Europe had state churches.

The U.S. Constitution made no mention of the relationship between church and state. Despite Washington's assurances, several leaders wanted a written guarantee of religious freedom. Thomas Jefferson, author of the Declaration of Independence, led the way with his Bill for Establishing Religious Freedom, which the Virginia legislature passed in 1786. It read in part:

"No man shall be compelled to frequent or support any religious worship, place, or ministry whatsoever, nor shall be enforced, restrained, molested, or burthened in his body or goods, nor shall otherwise suffer, on account of his religious opinions or belief; but that all men shall be free to profess, and by argument to maintain, their opinions in matters of religion."[9]

Patrick Henry, the Revolutionary firebrand who had demanded liberty or death, held a different view. He proposed a bill to Congress that declared Chris-

tianity as the national religion. But James Madison fought off Henry's efforts, which he viewed as "a dangerous abuse of power." [10]

Another factor weighed heavily against efforts to name a national religion: There were too many religions to establish one of them as the state church. At the urging of Jefferson and Madison, the young nation passed the First Amendment to the Constitution, which guaranteed religious freedom. It began, "Congress shall make no law respecting an establishment of religion, or prohibiting the free exercise thereof . . ."

It wasn't until 1815, however, that the state of Connecticut agreed to stop funding the Congregational Church. Massachusetts, the original Puritan strong-

James Madison: "The Religion then of every man must be left to the conviction and conscience of every man; and it is the right of every man to exercise it as these may dictate. This right is in its nature an unalienable right."[11]

hold, took another fifteen years before strong criticism from other churches forced the state to abandon its favoritism of the Congregational Church.

Before and during the American Revolution, thousands of people loyal to England fled the United States into Canada. Many of them were Anglicans, members of the Church of England.

The Anglicans who stayed in the United States, particularly in the South, made it clear their sympathies were with the colonists, not with England. In 1785, they formed the Protestant Episcopal Church of America and became known as Episcopalians.

The large influx of Anglicans into Canada gave Protestants there much more power. Even so, Canadian leaders realized the folly of forcing the entire population to embrace the Protestant Church. Sixty thousand Canadians of French descent, 90 percent of whom were Roman Catholic, were firmly entrenched in the fertile lands of Quebec.[12] They would never consent peacefully to abandon their faith. The Quebec Act of 1774 granted religious freedom to all Canadians.

By the end of the eighteenth century, Canada and the United States had firmly established the separation of church and state. In both nations, people of all religions were free, by law, to practice their faiths. Some sects continued to be persecuted; some government actions favored one religion over the other. But the tradition of religious tolerance had become part of the national identity of both nations.

Unlike their neighbors to the north, the Spanish and Portuguese colonies had few religions within their borders. After the conquering Spaniards and Portuguese suppressed the wide diversity of religions practiced by the native tribes, Roman Catholicism became the area's only official religion. A few scattered pockets of Protestants and followers of other faiths lived in areas settled by the British: Belize (then known as British Honduras), the Bahamas, Jamaica, and other island colonies. Workers imported from India, then part of the British Empire, brought Hinduism and Islam to Suriname (formerly Dutch Guiana), Trinidad and Tobago, and Guyana (formerly British Guiana).

From the start, the Spanish and Portuguese colonial governments worked hand in hand with the Roman Catholic Church in Latin America. Priests and bishops served as advisers to the colonial governors. Church courts tried offenders. The government collected fees for the church, paid its expenses, and often appointed bishops and archbishops. The king of Spain granted huge tracts of land to Catholic orders for their missions and churches.

While most bishops and archbishops in Latin America were Spanish-born and supported Spain's claim to its New World colonies, many of the lower-level priests, friars, and monks sided with the independence movement that began to take shape in the early 1800s.

Two Catholic priests took the lead in early efforts to win freedom in Mexico. On September 16, 1810, the bell rang loudly at the parish church in Dolores, a small village in central Mexico. At the signal, the villagers gathered around the parish's fifty-seven-year-old priest, Father Miguel Hidalgo y Costilla. Indians, mestizos (people of mixed Indian and Spanish blood), and creoles (American-born Spaniards) listened as he urged them to take up arms against the Spanish officials who oppressed them.

For several months, Hidalgo and a group of army officers, intellectuals, former officials, and other clergy had been plotting to overthrow the government in Mexico City. Now the priest's fiery words set off a storm of violence. Fighting under the banner of Our Lady of Guadalupe, the Indians—seething with rage over their unjust treatment by the Spaniards—ransacked villages, burned homes, and looted businesses. They attacked creoles and mestizos as well as Spaniards; whites were the enemy in their eyes.

Sickened by the race riots that had been set off, Hidalgo's coconspirators soon abandoned him. On January 17, 1811, a well-disciplined force of several thousand creoles and Spaniards defeated Hidalgo's much larger army and forced the priest into hiding. Captured in March, Hidalgo was jailed, deprived of his priestly robes, and shot to death on July 31, 1811.

José María Morelos, a priest and a follower of Hidalgo, took charge of the few remaining rebel forces. A capable leader, Morelos led the rebels on raids against the Spanish and won the support of most of the parish priests in southern Mexico. A rebel congress drew up its own constitution, demanding an end to slavery, independence from Spain, and abolishment of unjust taxes. It also called for the rebel state to operate as a Catholic nation. But by November 1815, the rebel army was on the run. Captured during a battle, Morelos was chained to a mule and taken to Mexico City. On December 22, 1815, the Spanish government ordered his execution.

The Spanish forces had put down the rebellion, but they couldn't silence the words that echoed through the hills and valleys of Mexico. Other liberators would heed the priests' call for freedom. In 1821, Mexico declared itself an independent nation.

By 1824, most of Spain's New World colonies had separated themselves from the European nation's control. Brazil, led by King Pedro I, declared its independence from Portugal in 1822.

FAVORED STATUS AND REPRESSION

During the Wars of Independence, some Latin American leaders turned against the Roman Catholic Church because of its association with the colonial government. The first president of the Argentine Republic, Bernardino Rivadavia, closed down monasteries and courts run by the church, ended state payments to support priests, and set up public schools. Chile's leader, Bernardo O'Higgins, restricted certain reli-

Simón Bolívar, a leader in the fight for South American independence: "The state cannot rule the conscience of the subjects, neither give an award or a punishment, because God is the only (higher) power."[13]

The majority of people in Latin America have clung to the Roman Catholic Church regardless of the support or disapproval of the government. Above, a religious festival in Minas Gerais, Brazil

gious processions and allowed non-Catholics to be buried in the nation's cemeteries. In Colombia, liberal leader José Hilario López lifted the requirement that people tithe, or give 10 percent of their earnings to the church. He also closed church courts, allowed divorce, and expelled an archbishop and two bishops. An 1853 law decreed that Colombian citizens had the right to practice the religion of their choice. The law marked the first time in Latin America that the church and state were officially separate.

Throughout the Wars of Independence and in the years that followed, the people of Latin America remained firmly Catholic. In almost all the new republics formed after the wars, Roman Catholicism eventually became the official religion. But the church also endured severe repression at the hands of those opposed to its power.

Depending on the faction in control of the government, new constitutions either gave the church special status or took away its privileges. Chile's O'Higgins was forced to resign amid controversy over his restrictions on the church. An 1833 constitution proclaimed Catholicism as the state church in Chile.

Likewise, Argentina's Rivadavia was driven from office; the church received government funds under an 1853 constitution. When liberals again resumed power in Argentina, they passed a law in 1884 that banned Roman Catholic clergy from teaching religion in public schools.

Colombians, under conservative rule, adopted a

new constitution in 1886 that reestablished Roman Catholicism as Colombia's official religion. The following year, Colombian leaders signed a pact with the Vatican to restore the Church's power.

Mexican President Benito Juárez, who had once studied to become a priest, issued reforms in 1858 that allowed freedom of religion, separated the church and the state, and ended state support of convents and monasteries. The reforms also required marriages, births, and deaths to be registered with the state; until then, the church had controlled such events. Under the new laws, the Catholic Church was allowed to own only places of worship; all other property was seized by the state.

Other Latin American nations followed a similar pattern. When conservatives were in power, the Catholic Church received favored status. Under liberal governments, the church's power was reduced.

Brazil's kings generally supported the Catholic Church. During a disagreement, however, King Pedro II jailed two bishops. When a coup took control and established the United States of Brazil in 1889, it declared that church and state would be separate. The church supported the move because it meant the government would no longer control its bishops or be able to interfere with church policy.

GROWTH AND CHANGE

Excitement gripped North America as it headed into the nineteenth century. Nurtured by the freedom guaranteed in the U.S. Constitution, religions flourished. In 1789 Congregational minister Jedidiah Morse noted that "since the war, a catholic, tolerant spirit . . . has greatly increased and is becoming universal."[1] In New York, dozens of churches of various denominations existed side by side. Among the congregations were eighty-seven English Presbyterian, sixty-six Dutch Reformed, thirty Baptist, twenty-six Episcopalian, twenty Quaker, twelve German Lutheran, two Moravian, one Methodist, one Roman Catholic, one Shaker, and one Jewish.[2]

No longer supported by the state, churches had to attract new members. The Louisiana Purchase, the huge tract of land purchased by the United States in 1803 from the French, doubled the size of the country and opened up new territory for the growing popula-

At left, an itinerant preacher rides through a rainstorm. These clergymen traveled in all kinds of weather to carry the teachings of the Protestant faith to pioneers settling along the U.S. frontier.

tion. This frontier, with pioneers pouring into the territory every day, presented the ideal opportunity for newer religions to recruit members. Methodists, Baptists, and Presbyterians led the way.

John Wesley, born in England and trained as an Anglican minister, founded the Methodist Episcopal Church in the United States in 1784. It was a straightforward Protestant faith that appealed directly to its followers to give up evil and love God. Wesley himself viewed it as a form of Anglicanism, but the Church of England rejected it because of disagreements over doctrine. Under Wesley's guidance, his followers formed societies and prayer groups. Itinerant preachers, some ordained by Wesley himself, rode on horseback along the American frontier, spreading the faith.

One of the most influential of the traveling preachers, Francis Asbury, was, like Wesley, born in England. He came to America as a missionary when he was twenty-six. In the following years, he traveled constantly, usually on horseback, from the East Coast to the Mississippi Valley, from Virginia and New England to the wilds of the American frontier. Known as the father of American Methodism, Asbury became the first bishop of the Methodist Episcopal Church.

The Baptists and the Methodists especially appealed to the rough-and-ready pioneers settling in the American West. Their preachers did not have to be college-educated; sometimes a farmer or a frontiersman filled the role, carrying a Bible as he went about his business. In an area with few organized churches, the pioneers welcomed the traveling preachers, who baptized their children and taught them Bible lessons, performed marriages, and oversaw funerals.

Presbyterians, who had formed their national organization in North America in 1787, sent their ministers to the frontier as well. Often one minister served two or three congregations. The Presbyterians introduced the camp meeting, where people from miles around camped and listened to preachers in the open air.[3] The Methodists and Baptists soon adopted the camp meetings, and the religious fervor spread faster.

The United States has had several religious revivals. In 1858 noonday prayer meetings in Boston and New York began attracting thousands. The movement spread to other cities, where people turned to religion to find answers to the problems of urban life. The powerful preacher Charles Finney was said to have converted fifty thousand people to Protestantism in one week.[4] So many people wanted to participate in the services that one church restricted speakers to "not more than two consecutive prayers or exhortations [earnest appeals]."[5]

NEW SECTS

Two new Protestant sects sprang from American soil during the 1800s: Christian Science and the Church of Jesus Christ of Latter-day Saints (the Mormons). Mary Baker Eddy founded Christian Science in Boston in 1879. The religious system urged followers to rely on faith, not drugs, to heal themselves. The church's teachings reawakened interest in natural treatment of disease; its giant publishing firm—owner of the *Christian Science Monitor,* among other publications—spread the sect's views worldwide. Eddy was ridiculed and opposed vehemently by the American medical community for her beliefs, but her sect gained strength, especially in cities.

The Mormons faced a more difficult time. Even in the tolerant atmosphere of the United States, they endured harassment and hatred from those who held opposing views. The Mormons based their faith on the Christian Bible and on visions reported by prophet Joseph Smith in the Book of Mormon, published in 1830. Smith announced in 1843 that he had had a revelation that allowed Mormon men to have more than one wife (polygamy). That practice, which a small number of Mormons adopted, clashed violently with the views of most Americans and led to discrimination against the entire sect.

Searching for a haven where they could practice their religion in peace, the Mormons trekked from New York to Ohio to Missouri. No state would allow them to settle. Missouri officials promised to exterminate them. In Illinois, an outraged mob dragged Joseph Smith from jail and murdered him. Fleeing further persecution, Mormon leader Brigham Young led his flock on a thousand-mile journey across the wilderness to Utah, then owned by Mexico. Arriving in July 1847, the sect settled in the Great Salt Lake Basin.

Immigrants seeking their fortunes or escaping persecution poured into North America, bringing new and old religions with them. The first big migration of Jews to North America came from Germany in the early 1800s. After the Civil War, from 1865 to 1915, Jews from many nations streamed into the United States. Most were Orthodox Jews, followers of the faith that dates back thousands of years and on which Christianity is based.

As the Jewish population grew, so did the Reform movement, a liberal form of Judaism created in Germany and first introduced to U.S. congregations in 1845 by Rabbi Isaac Mayer Wise. Reacting against the liberalism of the Reform movement, a group of American Jews led by Solomon Schechter urged a less radical approach. The new form of Judaism, known as Conservative, called for reforms that would enable Jews to adapt to American life. But Conservatism also kept much of the Jewish tradition, including the primary role of the Torah, the collection of Jewish laws and religious teachings.

In the 1840s, tens of thousands of Roman Catholics fleeing the potato famine in Ireland and bad economic conditions in France and other Roman Catholic nations streamed into the country. The sudden surge of Roman Catholic immigrants posed a threat to Protestants who wanted their religion to be the majority faith in America. Samuel F. B. Morse, inventor of the tele-

A Simple Life

For four hundred years, the Mennonites and the Amish have clung to traditions far removed from the everyday world.

Menno Simons, a Roman Catholic priest, founded the Mennonite sect in the 1500s in the Netherlands. Members live simple lives in communities based on farming, wear plain clothes, and rely on the Bible to guide believers. The group does not believe in private insurance and does not participate in the federal Social Security program. Instead, members take care of each other in times of trouble. Most Mennonites do not participate in competitive sports, own television sets, or sunbathe in public. They shun politics and refuse to serve in the military.

A group of six Mennonites, fleeing persecution in Germany, accepted William Penn's offer of refuge on eighteen thousand acres of land in Pennsylvania and sailed to the New World in 1683. Another group of Mennonites migrated west from Switzerland between 1810 and 1830, settling in Ohio and Indiana. In 1870, when Russia threatened to change the laws that exempted the large Mennonite community there from serving in the military, thousands moved to Manitoba and Kansas. Five or six thousand Mennonites from Canada, the United States, Russia, and Manchuria settled in Paraguay in the 1920s.

The Amish, a conservative offshoot of the Mennonite faith founded by Swiss Mennonite minister Jacob Amman, began their journey from Switzerland and Germany to America in 1727, followed by another migration in the 1740s. Most settled in Pennsylvania. The Amish reject modern life altogether. They travel in horse-drawn buggies, use animals instead of machinery to farm their lands, and fasten their clothing with hooks and eyes instead of "new fangled" buttons. Worship services are held in homes.

graph, urged Congress to halt immigration altogether, claiming Catholicism was "opposed in its very nature to Democratic Republicanism."[6]

Nativists—those who wanted to exclude everyone not born in America—formed the American or Know-Nothing Party to promote their views in Congress. In 1844, hoodlums burned a seminary and two Catholic churches in Philadelphia. A convent in Boston met a similar fate, and anti-Catholic mobs threatened violence in New York. The threats had little effect on the growing Catholic population. By 1850, Roman Catholicism claimed more members than any other church in America.[7] And the nation's attention was soon diverted from Catholicism to slavery.

Ironically, the real "natives"—American Indians—found themselves more unwelcome than the immigrants who sailed from foreign shores. Many of the Indians had long practiced Christianity and had adopted the lifestyles and customs of the Americans around them. But that wasn't enough to protect them. At President Andrew Jackson's bidding, Congress passed an Indian Removal Act in 1830 requiring all Indian tribes east of the Mississippi to move west.

U.S. Representative Edward Everett, a Unitarian minister from Massachusetts, berated Congress for its unfair treatment of the tribes. Samuel A. Worcester, a Congregational missionary to the Cherokees, took the issue to the U.S. Supreme Court and won, but President Jackson ignored the ruling. From 1830 to 1842, sixty thousand members of the Chickasaw, Seminole,

Creek, Choctaw, and Cherokee tribes were forced from their homes in the southeast to the wilds of the Oklahoma Territory.

By the end of the nineteenth century, almost all the tribes in the United States had been forced onto reservations. Some clung to Christianity; others practiced the ancient faiths of their ancestors.

THE SLAVERY ISSUE

Just as religious freedom didn't apply to everyone, freedom itself didn't apply to black slaves. Brought to the Western Hemisphere in chains, slaves were not allowed to have their own priests or to practice their own organized religion.

In both North America and Latin America, however, slaves were able to preserve many of their African religious traditions through ritual dances. Slave owners banned all other African rituals but allowed the dances because they thought the spirited movements were only for fun. Many slaves also retained their belief in spirits, or gods, that controlled nature. They taught their children many of these beliefs and the rituals, dances, and music brought from their African homeland.

In the United States, laws in the South banned whites from teaching slaves to read the Bible. Black household servants, however, sometimes accompanied their masters to Christian churches, though usually they were seated separately from whites. For many slaves, Christianity was a source of comfort that helped them endure their suffering.

The slavery issue split religious institutions down the middle, as it would the nation. As the controversy over slavery heated up, several religious leaders led the battle against the practice. Presbyterian minister Elijah Lovejoy printed a newspaper in St. Louis that called for the abolition of slavery. In 1837, a mob destroyed his press and shot him to death. Other church leaders helped slaves escape through an Underground Railroad, a secret network of hiding places, that led them from the South to safe havens in the North.

Northern churches hosted lecturers who spoke forcefully against slavery. Other Christian churches, particularly in the South, supported slavery. John England, a Roman Catholic bishop in South Carolina, described slavery as a system that protected blacks and provided them a livelihood.[8] Protestant preachers defended slavery in their sermons.

As the conflict intensified, so did the tension between northern and southern members of abolitionist and proslavery churches. In 1844, the Methodist Episcopal Church and the Methodist Episcopal Church, South, split over the slavery issue. They would not reunite until 1939. The Baptists followed suit in 1845. One hundred and fifty years later, delegates to the conservative Southern Baptist Convention, which remains separated from more moderate Baptist groups, joined hands and apologized for the organization's defense of slavery in the past.

Frederick Douglass, an escaped slave and a leading abolitionist: "While America is printing tracts and Bibles; sending missionaries abroad to convert the heathen; expending her money in various ways for the promotion of the Gospel in foreign lands, the slave not only lies forgotten—uncared for, but is trampled under foot by the very churches of the land."[9]

At right, a black minister visits members of his congregation in the South around the end of the nineteenth century.

War between the states broke out in 1861. The following year, President Abraham Lincoln issued the Emancipation Proclamation freeing the slaves, a move backed vigorously by the Committee from the Religious Denominations of Chicago, the American Baptist Home Mission Society, and other religious groups.

In the aftermath of the Civil War, churches on both sides of the conflict rallied to help those devastated by the war. Northern churches led the effort to aid freed blacks. The task was overwhelming. By 1875, five million former slaves—one-eighth of the U.S. population—needed training or help in getting established.[10] Churches provided food, clothing, and shelter and set up schools and religious instruction. Howard University, founded by the Freedmen's Bureau, prepared black men to become preachers.

Blacks flocked to newly created black churches,

most of which were patterned on Christian denominations. Northern blacks attended African Methodist Episcopal and African Methodist Episcopal Zion churches; in the South, the Colored Methodist Episcopal Church served black members. The African Methodist Episcopal, the first American church for blacks, had been founded in 1816 by Richard Allen, a slave who had won his freedom.

Black Baptist churches experienced the largest growth by far. In 1900, an estimated two million people were members of black Baptist churches. Another 1.1 million blacks attended related denominations.[11]

"Showplace of Religious Freedom"

The push west began again in earnest after the Civil War, and with it came America's introduction to the religions of Asia. Thousands of Chinese, who practiced Confucianism and Buddhism, migrated to the West Coast in the mid-1800s to escape wars in their homeland. They worked on the first transcontinental railroad, which opened up the vast lands of the West and Southwest in 1869.

Japanese Buddhists migrated from the Hawaiian Islands and settled along the U.S. western coast. Adding to the mix were Catholic immigrants newly arrived from Europe and Protestants from the East Coast, all lured west by the promise of gold and free land.

The Eastern Orthodox Church, a Christian church with national branches based in Greece, Russia, and

Above, a Greek Orthodox priest in Waterloo, Iowa, in 1915

eastern Europe, established a stronghold in Alaska. The Russians first established an Eastern Orthodox Church in the New World after staking claim to Alaska (Russian America) in 1741. By 1867, when Russia sold Alaska to the United States, about one-sixth of the population belonged to the Russian Orthodox Church.[12] Strengthened by immigrants from Ukraine, Russia, and the Baltic region, the Russian Orthodox Church numbered almost half a million members by 1916.[13] A similar surge of immigrants from Greece beginning in the 1890s bolstered the membership of the Greek Orthodox Church.

In the East, intellectuals dabbled in the philosophies of other cultures. Essayist-poet Ralph Waldo Emerson preached self-reliance, while men like educator-philosopher Amos Bronson Alcott (father of author Louisa May Alcott) set up communes in an effort to create a utopia, the perfect society.

A World Parliament of Religions, organized by Congregational minister John Henry Barrows in Chicago in 1893, focused attention on a myriad of religions unknown to most Americans. Speakers unfolded the mysteries of Buddhism, Hinduism, Confucianism, Shinto, and Islam to eager American audiences. Judaism, Roman Catholicism, Greek Orthodoxy, and the Protestant denominations also had presentations at the conference. Following the convention, a sect of Islam attracted a following in the Chicago area.[14] By 1900, notes historian Edwin Gaustad, the United States was "a showplace of religious freedom."[15]

The nineteenth century was a time of tremendous growth and change for Canada, as well. Through agreement with Great Britain, Canada became an independent commonwealth in 1867. Two years later, the Hudson's Bay Company, a British firm, sold Canada a huge tract of land that would later become the provinces of Manitoba, Alberta, and Saskatchewan. As in the United States, the nation's transcontinental railroad linked the east and west coasts in 1885. The discovery of gold in the Yukon in 1896 brought hordes of adventurers to western Canada.

The 1800s also brought bitter disputes between Canada's French-speaking Catholics and English-speaking Protestants. The conflict between Protestants and Catholics reached the boiling point in 1890 when the province of Manitoba cut off funds to French-speaking, Catholic schools. Since its founding in 1871, Manitoba had paid for both Catholic and Protestant schools, both of which served as the public school system. With the influx of new settlers, Protestants outnumbered Catholics in Manitoba by nine to one by 1890.[16]

Responding to Protestant voters, the legislators set up a new English-only school system that avoided religious teachings. The action set off an uproar among Canada's Catholic citizens of French descent. Finally, in 1896, Wilfrid Laurier, the nation's first French-Canadian prime minister, arranged a compromise.

Under its terms, Manitoba set up the school system as proposed but allowed schools in French-speaking areas to teach religion and French.

While relations between Catholics and Protestants remained strained, the various Protestant churches in Canada were moving together. Methodists in two branches of the church reunited in 1833, and all the branches of the denomination joined together in 1884 under the Methodist Church of Canada. Canadian Protestants consolidated even more in 1925 when Methodists, Presbyterians, and Congregationalists formed the United Church of Canada. Some Presbyterians, however, still operate as a separate church.

At the turn of the century, Canada, like the United States, became a destination for people seeking a haven from persecution. In 1898, the Doukhobors, also known as spirit wrestlers, fled from Russia to Canada. Settling in Saskatchewan and British Columbia, the sect practiced a mystical religion that rejected all rituals and relied on a holy spirit residing within believers. Members were pacifists; they believed disputes between nations could be settled peaceably rather than by war or violence. As pacifists, they refused to serve in the military. They also declined to send their children to public schools.

Ironically, the Indians, the area's original inhabitants, found no refuge in Canada. Their treatment was less brutal there than in the United States. But gradually the Canadian government forced the tribes onto reservations, where many of their descendants still live.

CHAPTER FIVE

RELIGION AND POLITICS

Beginning in the 1600s, public schools in North America had reflected the teachings of the Protestant religion. By the 1800s, Catholics, Jews, and those of other faiths in the United States had begun to question this practice. They argued that the First Amendment guaranteed that state (including public-financed schools) and church be separate. In *Minor v. Board of Education*, a court case filed in 1869, Jewish parents objected to the reading of the Protestant Bible in their child's public school. The Ohio Supreme Court agreed. In his opinion on the *Minor* case, Judge Alphonso Taft, father of the future president, noted that the Constitution did not permit schools run and paid for by the government to promote "Protestant worship."[1] The use of such rituals, he wrote, made it appear that the government favored the Protestant religion; that offended Catholics and Jews, who held other faiths.

RELIGION, MONKEYS, AND THE FIRST AMENDMENT

In 1925, the state of Tennessee took high school biology teacher John Scopes to court for teaching evolution—Charles Darwin's theory that plants and animals (including people) are descended from preexisting life forms. According to state law, it was illegal for teachers "to teach the theory that denies the story of the divine creation of man as taught in the Bible, and to teach instead that man has descended from a lower order of animals."

Lawyer Clarence Darrow argued that the law violated the First Amendment of the U.S. Constitution because it promoted the teachings of one religion (Christianity). "The State of Tennessee," Darrow told the jury, "has no more right to teach the Bible as the Divine Book than that the Koran is one, or the Book of Mormon, or the Book of Confucius, or the Buddha, or the Essays of Emerson, or any one of the 10,000 books to which human souls have gone for consolation and aid in their troubles."

William Jennings Bryan, the state's lawyer, contended that the evolution theory should not be taught because it contradicted the religious beliefs of most of the parents who paid to support the public schools. "Can a minority in this State come in and compel a teacher to teach that the Bible is not true and make the parents of these children pay the expenses of the teacher to tell their children what these people believe is false and dangerous?"

The jury agreed with Bryan and fined Scopes $100. The Tennessee Supreme Court later overturned the conviction because of a technicality. In 1968, the U.S. Supreme Court struck down a similar law in Arkansas because it violated the First Amendment. Conservative Christians today continue to fight against the teaching of evolution in public schools.

—From *A Documentary History of Religion in America Since 1865*

Since that case, courts have heard thousands of suits on the religious rights of Americans. The U.S. Supreme Court outlawed prayer in public school in the *Engel v. Vitale* case, decided on June 25, 1962. The High Court has also prohibited Bible reading, the Lord's Prayer, and most aid to church schools. In 1985, the Court ruled that a moment of silence (instead of prayer) could not be enforced at schools.

The Canadian Constitution guarantees the freedom of conscience and religion. Like the United States, Canada has no state religion.

The separation of church and state in the United States and Canada has not meant that religion and politics don't mix. In many ways, political rallies, where orators speak in fiery terms of their opponents' sins, resemble the religious camp meetings of the 1700s.

When Al Smith ran as the Democratic candidate for U.S. president in 1928, he noted, "I can think of no greater disaster to this country than to have the voters of it divide upon religious lines. It is contrary to the spirit, not only of the Declaration of Independence, but of the Constitution itself."[2] Opponents, nevertheless, made his Catholic religion a major issue, and Smith lost by a landslide. In the 1960 U.S. presidential election, opponents suggested John F. Kennedy, also a Catholic, might take orders from the pope. Kennedy quickly denied the charge and won in a close race against Richard Nixon.

In Canada, religion has played a role in the continuing conflict between French-speaking Catholics

Above, supporters of granting U.S. women the right to vote march down Fifth Avenue in New York City in 1915. Quakers were well represented in the effort.

and English-speaking Protestants. In Quebec, Canada's only French-Catholic province, citizens have long pushed for more power in running their province. Their desire to preserve their French-Catholic culture has led to two votes on Quebec's proposal to separate from Canada. In 1996 supporters of Quebec's independence lost by a margin of less than 1 percent.

Religious leaders have always been among those seeking social change. Quakers Lucretia Mott and Susan B. Anthony led the fight for women's rights in the United States in the second half of the 1800s. The Methodist societies formed by John Wesley earlier in the century played prominent roles in a number of social causes. A group of Methodist women knelt in front of an Ohio tavern in 1873 and prayed that the alcohol inside be destroyed. That action led a year later to the formation of the Women's Christian Temperance Union, which along with Baptists and others played a major role in banning the sale of alcohol in the United States with the passage of the Prohibition Act in 1919. Similar groups supported Canada's ban on alcohol sales during World War I.

Methodist and other church groups also helped win support for laws banning child labor and sweatshops in the United States and backed labor unions.

Rabbi Samuel Mayerberg battled corruption during Thomas Pendergast's administration in Kansas City, Missouri. From 1916 until he was jailed for tax evasion in 1939, Pendergast served as the powerful head of Kansas City's Democrats.

Protestant, Catholic, and Jewish leaders were behind the peace movement that flourished after World War I. In more recent times, Catholic priest Robert Drinan served in the U.S. House of Representatives in the 1960s and was a forceful critic of U.S. military policy during the Vietnam War. Former Roman Catholic priest Philip Berrigan continues to protest against nuclear weapons.

In the 1980s North American religious leaders helped more than half a million refugees escape from political unrest in Central America. Baptists, Lutherans, Presbyterians, Methodists, Society of Friends (Quakers), Roman Catholics, Jews, and members of the United Church of Christ and the Disciples of Christ (both Protestant sects) took part in the sanctuary movement. Almost one hundred church workers were arrested for hiding illegal aliens.[3]

THE PUSH FOR BLACK EQUALITY

Among the most noted American religious activists in the twentieth century was the Reverend Martin Luther King Jr., a black Baptist minister who spearheaded the civil rights movement in the 1960s. He preached nonviolent resistance to further the rights of black Americans.

For many black Americans in the United States, however, Christianity represented slavery and the repression of their race. Some black Christian leaders preached of a black Mary giving birth to a black Christ.

Dr. Martin Luther King Jr.: "I have a dream that one day every valley shall be exalted, every hill and mountain shall be made low, the rough places will be made plains, and the crooked places will be made straight, and the glory of the Lord shall be revealed, and all flesh shall see it together."[4]

Others urged their followers to reject Christianity altogether and its "white Gods." Responding to the growing discontent of blacks over their treatment in a segregated America, Wallace D. Fard founded the Temple of Islam in Detroit in 1930. Fard, who went by the name of Wali Farad Muhammad, based his ministry on that of Timothy Drew, a black North Carolina preacher who had studied Islam.

Robert Poole took over the Chicago ministry after Fard disappeared in 1934. Taking the name Elijah Muhammad, the young Georgian, whose father had been a Baptist minister, rejected Christianity and established the Nation of Islam. He taught that American blacks were descended from an ancient tribe of Shabazz that traced its roots to Abraham and that Caucasians, those with white skin, were inferior.

Elijah's message attracted a huge following among the angry young black men caught in the turmoil of the civil rights movement. Followers were informally known as Black Muslims, because they followed Islamic doctrine. Many traditional Muslims, however, objected to the label because of Elijah's racist message.

Malcolm X, born Malcolm Little, the son of a Baptist preacher, became the movement's best-known spokesman. After a dispute with Elijah, Malcolm X formed his own organization, which he called the Organization of Afro-American Unity. Claiming to be a traditional Muslim, Malcolm X preached a moralistic code: no alcohol or drugs, responsible behavior, hard work, and respect for women. He also abandoned his

CELEBRATING KWANZA

Kwanza is a holiday created specifically for blacks in the United States. It has many of the elements of religious thought and ritual, but it is not tied to any particular religion. Blacks of many faiths celebrate the holiday, which honors African-American heritage.

Kwanza evolved from the U.S. civil rights movement of the 1960s. It attempts to preserve the rites transported from the African homeland of the slaves.

The seven-day holiday, an invention of civil rights activist Maulana Karenga, is celebrated from December 26 to January 1. It is based on seven principles of behavior: unity, self-determination, collective work and responsibility, cooperative economics, purpose, creativity, and faith.

During Kwanza ceremonies, celebrants place gifts of fruits, nuts, and corn and other vegetables, on a festive mat. Corn represents children and symbolizes the need to care for the young. The other gifts of food are reminders of African harvest festivals.

Many of the rites focus on family. Everyone shares a meal, called karamu, that features African specialties. Names of black heroes are read; members of the group pass around a Unity Cup and take turns describing what the holiday means to them. On the last day of Kwanza, children are given gifts that represent the seven principles.

In creating the holiday, Karenga noted that Kwanza provided "a Black alternative to the existing holiday [Christmas] and [gave] Blacks an opportunity to celebrate themselves."

An estimated eighteen million black Americans—including many Christians who also observe Christmas—celebrate the holiday.

—From *Harper's Magazine*

call for a separate black nation in favor of a socialist state of both blacks and whites. On February 21, 1965, a gunman shot and killed Malcolm X in New York City.

Black leader Louis Farrahkan now heads the Nation of Islam. On October 16, 1995, Farrahkan organized a massive Million Man March in Washington, D.C. Between 400,000 and 800,000 black men attended the peaceful rally, the largest gathering of blacks in U.S. history. At the march, Farrahkan called on participants to be proud of their race, to assume their role as responsible fathers and husbands, and to spurn violence, drugs, and child and spouse abuse. Farrahkan is a controversial figure, however, because of verbal attacks against white people, Catholics, and Jews that have been attributed to him.

POLITICAL ORGANIZATIONS

Some religious groups—Fundamentalist Christians (conservative Protestants) in particular—have set up full-fledged political organizations to take stands on issues and lobby for laws that favor their views. The Fundamentalists' political efforts began in earnest in the United States in 1979 when the Reverend Jerry Falwell founded the Moral Majority. Among the causes the organization backed were prayer in public schools, increased military spending, and the teaching of the Bible's version of creation. The group opposed abortion, homosexuality, pornography, and the failed Equal Rights Amendment that would have granted women equal legal status in the U.S. Constitution. In 1980, the Moral Majority formed a powerful voting bloc when its four million members helped Ronald Reagan win his race for the U.S. presidency. The group disbanded in 1989, but similar groups, such as the Christian Coalition, have taken its place.

Like the Protestant Fundamentalists, the Roman Catholic Church has lobbied hard against abortion and birth control. Other religious groups, including Unitarians, Jews, and most mainstream Protestant denominations, have supported birth control and the right of a woman to have an abortion. They have also opposed censorship and school prayer.

Though members of different religions disagree on a number of issues, religious leaders have begun to focus on the things that unite them. Protestant and Catholic churches joined together in the World Council of Churches, founded in 1948, and the National Council of Churches, established in the United States in 1950. Eastern Orthodox churches made moves to join under one banner. Their leaders also began talks with Anglicans. Catholics, Protestants, and Jews have participated in meetings to further understanding.

ACTIVIST PRIESTS OF LATIN AMERICA

On Sunday, March 23, 1980, Oscar Romero, archbishop of San Salvador, the capital of El Salvador, made a radio broadcast to the soldiers fighting in the name of his tiny Central American country.

In 1994, the Christian Coalition helped conservative Republicans who shared their views on school prayer and other issues win seats in the U.S. House of Representatives and the Senate.

"Soldiers," the archbishop pleaded, "do not obey your superiors when they order you to kill. You are killing your brothers and sisters. In the name of God, in the name of these suffering people whose laments rise to heaven, each day more tumultuous, I beg of you, I ask of you, I order you, in the name of God, stop the repression!"[5]

For a dozen years, the Salvadoran army, financed with U.S. aid, waged war on left-wing guerrillas opposed to the El Salvador government. During the conflict, which did not end until 1992, more than seventy-five thousand people were killed. Most of the dead were civilians. Romero and other religious leaders protested the government's repressive tactics—torture of citizens to gain information about guerrillas, censorship of the press, death squads—and called for an end to the war.

The day after Romero's broadcast, he stood in the chapel of a cancer hospital saying Mass in memory of a woman who had died. As Romero administered the sacrament, shots echoed through the room. The archbishop fell to the floor, his body crumpled beneath a crucifix on the wall in back of him. Women who had crouched in the pews at the sound of the guns ran to the archbishop and gently turned him onto his back. The bullet had entered near his heart. Blood covered his robe. Romero died as emergency workers tried in vain to give him a blood transfusion.

Priests, friars, and other religious leaders have often taken courageous stands against governments in their efforts to protect their congregation and their faith. The Jesuits armed the Indians in their care and taught them to fight off slave-hunters. In the early 1800s, Franciscan Friar Luís Beltrán manufactured cannons for the freedom fighters in Peru from the bells of his parish church.

For most of the Latin American nations, the battle for independence was followed by years of unrest. Dictators, military coups, and unscrupulous leaders took turns wresting control of the government. The people lived in poverty and fear. During this time, the region's religious leaders—most of whom were Catholic—witnessed the injustice and the atrocities. Many became convinced that their role as priests demanded that they do something to help the people caught in the horrors of political turmoil. Out of this conviction came liberation theology, the belief that Christian teachings demand that Christians do what they can to bring about social justice.

Liberation theology is tied to the reforms of the Second Vatican Council, a meeting of Roman Catholic bishops and other officials worldwide held from 1962 to 1965. The reforms, initiated by Pope John XXIII, aimed at increasing the Catholic Church's involvement with the poor. For some priests, social action meant joining forces with left-wing guerrilla groups or supporting the struggle of the working class. Others worked with peace groups or other social action organizations. Because they tried to change conditions, most of the activist priests ran afoul of their government. Two Argentine priests lost their jobs after they supported students who were protesting a military coup. In Brazil, hundreds of priests opposed to the government there were thrown in jail. Some, like Romero, became martyrs to the cause.

Church leaders have not always supported the actions of liberation priests. Pope John Paul II forced Jean-Bertrand Aristide, president of Haiti, to leave the priesthood when his activities became too political. Some fear the activists are helping Communist forces take over Latin American countries.

Priests travel a fine line between political and social action in Latin America today. They continue their work to help the poor, but many avoid political activities. The National Council of Brazilian Bishops, for example, voted against supporting political parties but voted to work for land reform and fair treatment of workers.[6]

In Cuba, Roman Catholics have endured the repression of a Communist regime headed by Fidel Castro. After Castro announced he had allied with the communist Soviet Union in 1961, Catholic schools were closed and church property was turned over to the state. Thousands of Cubans fled their island home with the help of Roman Catholic clergy. Roman Catholics were kept out of Cuban politics; they were banned from the Communist Party, and their charitable work in schools, hospitals, and jails was limited. The press, censored by Castro's government, was not permitted to report on the works of the church.

In 1960 745 Roman Catholic priests and 2,225 members of Roman Catholic religious orders served Cuba.[7] By 1970 only 250 priests and 450 nuns carried on the administration of the church in Cuba after Castro restricted the number of foreign religious people allowed into the country.[8] Despite the obstacles, Cubans clung to their faith.

Today, Castro has reached a more moderate approach to the church. A 1992 change in the Cuban Constitution bans religious discrimination. Church members can now join the Communist Party and face fewer restrictions. In turn, the Catholic Church has modified its opposition to Castro's Cuba. In 1996, the Vatican criticized a U.S. ban on trade with Cuba. Late in the year, Castro met with Pope John Paul II at the Vatican in Rome. At that meeting, the pope accepted Castro's invitation to visit Cuba in 1998. For both the church and Castro, the visit signals a new beginning.

Above, a Mayan temple in Chiapas, Mexico

A VITAL FORCE

Religion today remains a vital force among the inhabitants of the Western Hemisphere. Everywhere one looks are reflections of the religions of the past and present: Mayan architecture in Mexico, the bright costumes of the Mardi Gras celebrants in Rio de Janeiro, the totem poles in northwestern Canada, the neat white churches in New England villages.

Even among those who do not profess a faith, religion affects their everyday lives. The laws, the consti-

Religion remains a vital force in the Western Hemisphere. Above, a Protestant minister greets his congregation.

tutions, the courts, and the calendar are all based on religious concepts. Religious leaders head movements aimed at social change. Church groups push governments to pass legislation. In some Latin American countries, such as Argentina, Costa Rica, and Bolivia, Roman Catholicism remains the official religion of the nation.

Religion in the Western Hemisphere has undergone profound changes since the first natives worshiped their gods. Christianity, transplanted from Europe, has become the principal religion of the Americas. The Roman Catholic Church claims more members in the Western Hemisphere than any other. The Protestant faith has grown from one denomination to hundreds; a few had their start on American soil. Jews, Muslims, Buddhists, Hindus, and others have all brought their religions to the New World.

Many of these people, transplants from Europe or other nations of the world, have modified their religious practices to fit life in their new homelands. The hemisphere's original inhabitants and the black slaves brought to the New World against their will continue to perform rites and recite myths passed down from their ancient traditions. All have contributed to the hybrid civilization that has evolved in the Western Hemisphere.

GLOSSARY

clan	a group of family members within a tribe
Communion	a Christian ritual that celebrates Christ's Last Supper; participants eat bread (symbolizing Christ's body) and drink wine or juice (symbolizing Christ's blood); also called the Eucharist
creationism	a belief held by conservative Christians that God created people in the form they exist today, as opposed to evolution
creole	a Spaniard born in the New World
deist	a person who believes in God but not in organized religion
evolution	a theory, first proposed by Charles Darwin, that earth's plants and animals, including humans, developed from simpler organisms over millions of years
fetish	an object believed to have power or influence with the gods
friar	a member of a Roman Catholic religious group, such as the Franciscans; many friars established missions in the New World
icon	a picture or an object representing a sacred person
kachina doll	a doll that represents a spiritual being in some Native American religions
liberation theology	the belief that Christian teachings demand that Christians do what they can to bring about social justice; practiced particularly by Roman Catholic priests in Latin America
loa	a collection of spirits in voodoo
mestizo	a Latin American of mixed Spanish and Indian ancestry
monk	a member of a Roman Catholic religious group, such as the Jesuits, who live in a monastery and follow certain cer-

tain rules that govern their lives; monks also established missions in the New World

myth   stories carried down from one generation to the next that illustrate a society's beliefs

Nativists   a nineteenth century political group that favored people born in the United States and opposed immigration into that country

New World   the term used by Europeans to refer to the Western Hemisphere; it was an ancient world to the natives, whose ancestors had migrated there thirty thousand years before Columbus's voyage

peyote   a hallucinogenic drug derived from cactus used in sacred ceremonies by members of the Native American Church

polygamy   having more than one wife or husband at one time; practiced by a small group of Mormons in the nineteenth and early twentieth centuries

rite   a formal ceremony followed in observing religious beliefs

sect   an independent religious group

serf   a person of the lowest classes required to work on the land of a European lord during the Middle Ages

shaman   a priest and medicine man among some North American Indian tribes

totem pole   a post carved with faces of animals or other images by Indians in northwestern North America; totem poles were believed to offer protection from harm

voodoo   a set of religious beliefs with roots in Africa; followers participate in rituals they believe allow them to contact the dead

SOURCE NOTES

INTRODUCTION: PART OF THE FABRIC OF LIFE

1. John Bierhorst, *The Mythology of Mexico and Central America* (New York: William Morrow, 1990), 206.

CHAPTER ONE: THE FIRST WORSHIPPERS

1. John Bierhorst, *The Mythology of North America* (New York: William Morrow, 1985), 48.

2. "Indians," *Compton's Encyclopedia*, vol. 25, (F.E. Compton Co., 1985), 141.

3. Ibid.

4. Edwin S. Gaustad, ed., *A Documentary History of Religion in America to the Civil War* (Grand Rapids, Mich: William B. Eerdmans Publishing Co., 1982), 5–8.

5. Joseph Bruchac, "Digging Into Your Heart," *Parabola*, Winter 1994, 40.

6. Geoffrey Parrinder, ed., *World Religions: From Ancient History to the Present* (New York: The Hamlyn Publishing Group Ltd., 1971), 88.

7. John Bierhorst, *The Mythology of Mexico and Central America*, 190.

CHAPTER TWO: EUROPEANS IN THE NEW WORLD

1. Sydney E. Ahlstrom, *A Religious History of the American People* (New Haven: Yale University Press, 1972), 37.

2. John Edwin Fagg, *Latin America: A General History*, 2nd ed. (New York: Macmillan, 1969), 176.

3. Ibid., 178.

4. Ahlstrom, *A Religious History of the American People*, 200.

5. Edwin S. Gaustad, ed., *A Documentary History of Religion in America to the Civil War*, 279.

6. Edwin Williamson, *The Penguin History of Latin America* (New York: Penguin Books, 1992), 173.

7. Ibid., 143.

8. Ahlstrom, *A Religious History of the American People*, 46.

8. Ibid., 262.

9. Ibid., 191.

10. Ibid.

11. Ibid., 135.

12. *The Religious History of New England* (Cambridge, Mass.: Harvard University Press, 1917), 13.

13. Gaustad, *A Documentary History of Religion in America Since 1865*, 436.

14. Ahlstrom, *A Religious History of the American People*, 166.

15. Ibid., 154.

16. Ibid., 200.

17. Gaustad, *A Documentary History of Religion in America to the Civil War*, 149.

18. Ahlstrom, *A Religious History of the American People*, 217.

CHAPTER THREE: REVIVAL AND REVOLUTION

1. Gaustad, *A Documentary History of Religion in America to the Civil War*, 194.

2. *The Religious History of New England*, 46.

3. Ibid., 46–47.

4. Ahlstrom, *A Religious History of the American People*, 287.

5. *The Religious History of New England*, 50.

6. Gaustad, *A Documentary History of Religion in America to the Civil War*, 194.

7. Ahlstrom, *A Religious History of the American People*, 294.

8. Gaustad, *A Documentary History of Religion in America to the Civil War*, 279.

9. Ibid., 261.

10. Ibid., 262.

11. Gaustad, *A Documentary History of Religion in America to the Civil War*.

12. Andrew H. Malcolm, *The Land and People of Canada* (New York: HarperCollins, 1991), 105–106.

13. Pedro Moreno, "Church and State in Latin American Constitutions (Media House International, web site: http://www.forerunner/X0246_Church_State_in_Con.html, November 1993).

CHAPTER FOUR: GROWTH AND CHANGE

1. Gaustad, *A Documentary History of Religion in America to the Civil War*, 307.

2. Ibid., 308.

3. Paul Hutchinson and Winfred E. Garrison, *20 Centuries of Christianity: A Concise History* (New York: Harcourt, Brace and Company, 1959), 238.

4. Gaustad, *A Documentary History of Religion in America to the Civil War*, 403.

5. Ibid., 404.

6. Ibid., 460.

7. Ibid., 414.

8. Gaustad, *A Documentary History of Religion in America to the Civil War*, 486.

9. Ibid., 473–474.

10. Gaustad, *A Documentary History of Religion in America Since 1865*, 27.

11. Ibid., 30.

12. Ibid., 77.

13. Ahlstrom, *A Religious History of the American People*, 72.

14. Ibid.

15. Gaustad, *A Documentary History of Religion in America Since 1865*, 4–5.

16. "Manitoba Schools Question," *The 1995 Grolier Multimedia Encyclopedia* (Grolier Electronic Publishing, Inc., 1995).

CHAPTER FIVE: RELIGION AND POLITICS

1. Gaustad, *A Documentary History of Religion in America Since 1865*, 50.

2. Ibid., 274–275.

3. Ann E. Weiss, *Good Neighbors? The U.S. and Latin America* (Boston: Houghton Mifflin Co., 1985), 107.

4. Garry Wills, *Under God: Religion and American Politics* (New York: Simon and Schuster, 1990), 204.

5. The Rev. Jorge Lara-Braud, "Oscar Romero: Beatitude Made Flesh" (The Protestant Hour, web site: http://www.prtvc.org, January 28, 1996).

6. Christopher Richard, *Cultures of the World: Brazil* (New York: Marshall Cavendish, 1991), 66.

7. Enrique Dussel, *A History of the Church in Latin America: Colonialism to Liberation* (Grand Rapids, Mich.: William B. Eerdmans Publishing Co., 1981), 162.

8. Ibid.

FURTHER READING

Clark, Brenda. *Fighting for Their Faith.* Chatham, N.J.: Raintree Steck-Vaughn Publishers, 1990.

Dudley, Mark E. *Engel v. Vitale (1962): Religion and the Schools.* New York: Twenty-First Century Books, 1994.

Enriquez, Edmund C. *The Gold Gospel: A Pictorial History of the Restoration.* Bountiful, Utah: Horizon Publishers & Distributors Inc., 1981.

Ganeri, Anita, and Marcus Braybrooke. *Religions Explained: A Beginner's Guide to World Religions.* New York: Henry Holt, 1997.

Gay, Kathlyn. *Communes and Cults.* New York: Twenty-First Century Books, 1997.

Gifford, D. *Warriors, Gods & Spirits From South American Mythology.* New York: Marshall Cavendish, 1996.

Heily, Mathilde, and Rémy Courgeon. *Montezuma and the Aztecs.* New York: Henry Holt, 1996.

Hevly, Nancy. *Preachers and Teachers.* New York: Twenty-First Century Books, 1995.

Langley, Myrtle. *Religion.* New York: Alfred A. Knopf, 1996.

Newman, Shirlee P. *The Incas.* New York: Franklin Watts, 1995.

Patterson, J. *Jewish Americans.* New York: Marshall Cavendish, 1995.

Pennock, Michael F. *The Catholic Church Story.* Notre Dame, Ind.: Ave Maria Press, 1991.

Sherrow, Victoria. *Separation of Church and State.* New York: Franklin Watts, 1992.

Sinnott, Susan. *Chinese Railroad Workers.* New York: Franklin Watts, 1994.

Van Steenwyk, Elizabeth. *The California Missions.* New York: Franklin Watts, 1995.

Wood, M. Spirits, *Heroes & Hunters From North American Indian Mythology.* New York: Marshall Cavendish, 1996.